We dedicate this book to our friend
Billy Stockman Tjapaltjarri

Margo and Janusz

Sturt's Desert Pea

JANUSZ B. KRECZMANSKI
&
MARGO STANISLAWSKA-BIRNBERG

"THE TJULKURRA"

BILLY STOCKMAN TJAPALTJARRI

J.B. BOOKS

J.B. BOOKS AUSTRALIA - 2002

"The Tjulkurra"
Billy Stockman Tjapaltjarri

This first edition is an exclusive production published in the year 2002
by J.B. Books Pty Ltd
P.O. Box 118
Marleston 5033
South Australia
Phone/Fax (08) 8297 1669

The authors wish to thank the owners of copyright for their kind permission to reproduce the images of paintings in this book.

National Library of Australia
Cataloguing in Publication data:

Kreczmanski, Janusz., Stanislawska-Birnberg, Margo
"The Tjulkurra" Billy Stockman Tjapaltjarri.

ISBN 1 876622 37 7

1. Aborigines, Australia-Poetry-Painting-Photography.
2. Painting, Modern-20th century-Australia.
3. Painting, Australian-Aboriginal artist-Biography.
4. Biography, Tjapaltjarri Billy Stockman.

Book design by: **J.B. Kreczmanski**
and **Margo Stanislawska-Birnberg**
Graphic design, editing: **J.B.Kreczmanski**
Assistance in computer graphics: **Les Pach**
Text editing: **Penelope Charlesworth**
Produced by **Phoenix Offset.**

CONTENTS

Ghost Gum

Introduction

Rock shelter at Ubirr

Ewaninga rock carvings

Paintings at Nourlangie

Human fascination with painting pre-dates written history. Ancient drawings, engravings and paintings found all around the world, in caves, grottoes or on rocks, generate interest to this day. Great collections of this kind of art when viewed at exhibitions in museums, show-cased in public buildings or displayed in private homes excite our imagination and evoke in us an emotional experience. We encounter the dawn of our own humanity. In this kind of art one can trace the development of different expressions of painting styles. But there is one kind of traditional painting which has not changed for thousands of years in its form and subject matter: the art of the Australian Aborigines.

Ewaninga rock carvings

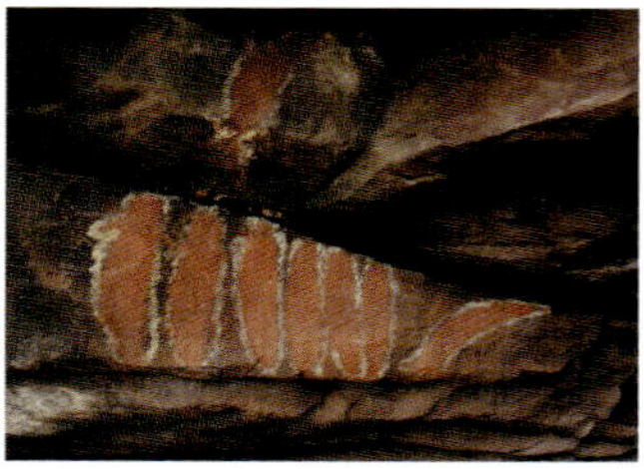

Arnhem Land, rock paintings.

On the Australian continent and its neighbouring islands, one finds large numbers of engravings, drawings and rock paintings executed by the indigenous population. Some of this art, dated by scientific methods, has been shown to be more than 40 000 years old. They are considered to be the first evidence of human art endeavours. Aborigines insist that Dreamtime ancestors made the oldest pecked-out designs and rock paintings. They had created the universe, the world and all the natural features. Many tribes call the beginning and the continuity of life "TJUKURRPA".

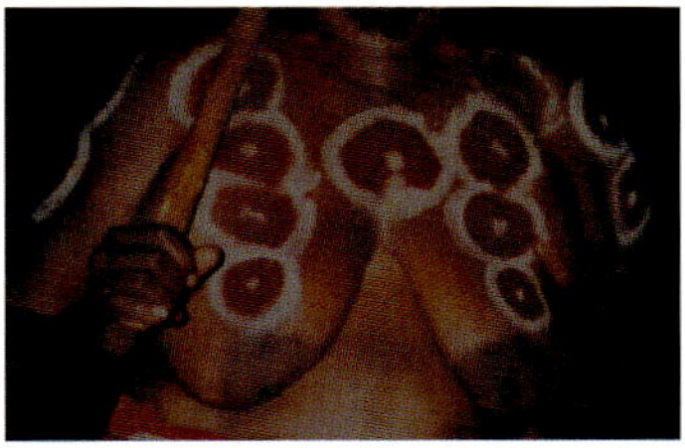

For thousands of years and to this day, the Australian Aborigines have painted, not only on rocks (the most durable medium) but also on bark stripped from trees, their bodies and on the ground. When "painting" on the ground dyed down, crushed or whole seeds, plants and sand mixed with ochres are used. In this way the Aborigines transform their stories into a visual language. It is a language, which is rich in legends, moral tales and histories of creation.

Sand painting

About thirty years ago an art teacher, Geoffrey Bardon, came to a desert settlement school in Papunya. At that time, in accordance with the prevailing government policy of assimilation of the Aboriginal people with the mainstream Australian population, the nomadic people were trucked from the desert areas and forcibly settled on reserves. Papunya was one of the places designated for the Warlpiri and Anmatyerre tribal Aborigines.

Geoffrey Bardon

Papunya was a dismal place. People who were used to open spaces and unimpeded movement between places found themselves virtual prisoners. Apathy reigned. The longing for the desert and past lifestyle found an outlet in sand drawings. To an inexperienced eye the marks drawn were idle doodling, but for tribal Aborigines they were the stories of creations. Bardon wanted to find out the meaning of the symbols painted by the desert people. He asked what they represented and why they used, for example, dots?

The tribal elders tried to satisfy Geoffrey's interest. It is they who are the most versed in secret tribal lore.

- *Can you see how the prickly spinifex grows and how it spreads on the red sand in rounded clumps?*

- *Did you observe the different tracks left by animals on the sand dunes?*

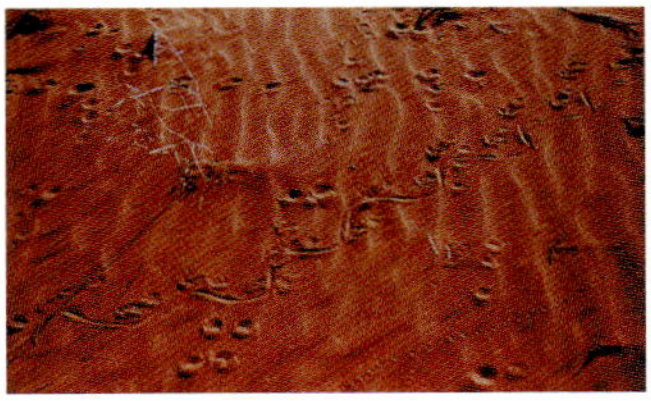

- *What kind of mark does a man leave after sitting down?*

- *Have you seen the curved tracks left by a slithering snake?*

- *Did you really look at the desert from a mountaintop?*

After some time Bardon persuaded a few of the elders to transfer the designs, which were traditionally painted on bodies or sand, onto more permanent medium. The shifting sands and the human body could not record for posterity the stories of ancient law called Tjukurrpa.

The men concerned were:

Kappa Mbitjana Jampitjinpa, Old Mick Jakamarra, Long Jack Philipus Jakamarra, Uta Uta Jangala, Billy Stockman Tjapaltjarri, and the youngest of the famous group Clifford Possum Tjapaltjarri.

The first tentative steps gave a new beginning to an explosion of expression, in new materials, for the oldest and at the same time the youngest art form practiced by humanity.

From these simple beginnings began a fantastic new movement of Aboriginal art, considered by art critics as the last important art movement at the end of the 20th century.

MacDonnell Ranges

Tanami Desert

Dingo

Billy Stockman Tjapaltjarri

THE TJULKURRA

The Tjulkurra's hair, his moustache and beard are white. His smile and friendly manner invites one for a conversation.

The Tjulkurra is very garrulous. He talks with great dignity and pronounces his words in clear English. He is not only well versed in his tribal language, Anmatyerre, but also several other Aboriginal languages.

While the Tjulkurra paints Dreamtime stories he sits on the red desert sand. At this moment he is very serious and collected. Sometimes, while painting, he sings the songs connected to the legends he is putting down on canvas.

The Tjulkurra - **BILLY STOCKMAN TJAPALTJARRI** is one of the most famous and prolific Australian painters.

"Tjulkurra", in the Anmatyerre language means, *"one with grey hair"*.

The Tjulkurra - Billy Stockman Tjapaltjarri.

Trachoma invading his eyes
Hands slowing down and stiffening
Legs too tired to carry his years
But the old Tjulkurra still has his smile.
Good morning, how are you?
Greets me every day
And when I recall the Anmatyerre word he taught me
He nods with approval his snow-white head.
Yowi, yes, you got that one,
Palya lingka, it's a good one, **he says**
Precious words from his childhood
Punctuate his proper sounding English accented speech.

But Billy's long life is still overshadowed
In remembrance of his younger days
When only just a baby
He survived a massacre in a coolamon hidden.
Dark days of 1928
When familiar sandhills reverberated to guns
Bad deeds in Coniston cannot be forgotten
Tribal members perished among the dunes.
Punitive posse with vengeful hearts
Galloped from distant place.

Unsuspecting and untroubled
Small family groups camped by a riverbed.
Children's laughter rang in clear desert air,
The smoke of fires rose high to the moon
Clapping of sticks and chanting of men
Mingled with sounds and smells of the bush.

Then shrieks and confusion.
Cries of lost children.
Hooves flailing.
Report of guns.
Pounding feet.
Dying and dead
Heaped on one bank.
Stench of burning flesh.
One small baby whimpering quietly
In bushes, hastily concealed by mother's loving care.

Margo Stanislawska-Birnberg.

Mt.Liebig, 1267m. MacDonnell Ranges

The survivor

Billy Stockman Tjapaltjarri was born around 1928 at a desert camp called Ilpitirri. By birth he is a member of the Anmatyerre tribe. The white people who were developing a cattle run on the traditional territories of the Anmatyerre people called it Mount Denison Station. At the very beginning of his life Billy was given a taste of the white men's "benevolence". In that fateful year, he and his family encountered the wrath of the white people. In August, the local Aborigines killed a white man, a dingo trapper who was shooting native dogs on the Anmatyerre's tribal territories. Brooks, as the white man was called, took advantage of an Aboriginal woman and ignored the woman's husband when asked to relinquish her. According to tribal law this kind of behaviour was not to be condoned. Retaliation followed swiftly.

A punitive expedition made up of volunteers, most of them local farmers under the command of a policeman, William George Murray, rode from Alice Springs 280km away, and swooped on the unsuspecting tribal people. Indiscriminate shooting followed and many were killed. Few were able to run away. Only those, who were at that time hunting or visiting other tribal groups survived.

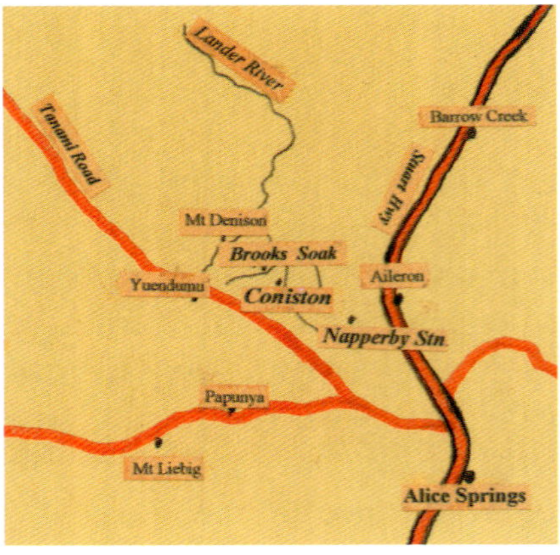

ONE newborn baby, sleeping in a coolamon thrust under a bush by his terrified mother, survived the massacre. It was Billy. His mother was not so lucky, her body falling on the river sand next to her family. No mercy was shown, as men, women and children fell under a volley of shots.

This infamous deed is now called "The Coniston Massacre" a name derived from the nearby cattle station, Coniston. The place where the mass murder happened now carries the name "Brook's Soak".

The small group that survived the massacre found shelter among Aborigines working at a neighbouring "Napperby Station". Billy was cared for and "adopted" into the family of One Pound Jimmy Tjungurrayi and Long Rose Nangala (the sister of Billy's mother). One Pound Jimmy was the father of Tim Leura Tjapaltjarri and Clifford Possum Tjapaltjarri. Tim and Clifford become very well known artists. Jimmy himself also achieved some fame when he was pictured on two Australian stamps issued on August 14, 1950. The adoptive parents of Billy took in another boy, Cassidy Tjapaltjarri. From then on Cassidy, Tim, Billy and Clifford were commonly considered "brothers".

Mt.Liebig – a desert settlement. Billy Stockman lives and paints here.

Amunurunga Range. Mt Liebig. Berry Pass valley.

A stockman and a sculptor

Billy spent his childhood and early adolescence with his new family. They moved between two cattle stations "Aileron" and "Napperby". Here he became initiated into the sacred, secret world of an Aboriginal man and a tribal member. It was also here, on one of the stations, that Billy got his first job as a stockman. He quickly learned English and after some time became very proficient in it.

During the past twelve years we have visited Billy frequently. In one of our conversations with him he sadly said:

- I was somebody when I worked as a stockman. Other people considered me. We, the working Aborigines were needed. I had special clothes; boots, hat…I liked working with cattle, branding them and looking for the stray ones in the bush. I loved riding. Life was hard but it was good. Then we lost our work. White station managers said they would not pay us white men's wages. No more cows and bullocks to brand. We were taken to settlements and were given "sit down money". Yes, that was bad. No work. Sit all day. Nothing, nothing…

Billy's friendly and outgoing personality made him very popular with many people. At the beginning of the 1949s he began to occupy himself with craft production. The free time between stock-work gave him the opportunity to make boomerangs and to carve figurines of animals out of wood. Later he started to draw and paint his first designs on boomerangs.

"LIZARD" a carving by Billy Stockman Tjapaltjarri.

After some time Billy became restless. The need to travel, to keep on the move and the desire to learn about other parts of world became very pervasive.

Droving cattle to the far north of the continent, where the American army was stationed, became an adventure in itself. Billy sold his boomerangs to the soldiers and from them he heard stories of other countries and different people. His curiosity was further aroused and he decided to see, at the least, a small part of the world beyond the seas.

From the end of the Second World War until the beginning of the 1960s, Billy, together with his "brothers" worked mainly as a stockman on the nearby cattle stations. Even then he never parted with his small knife with which he kept carving lizards, snakes, kangaroos and boomerangs. Some of the carvings he sold to tourists but most he gave away. He was happy with the thought that his carvings were appreciated and liked by others.

In the late 1960s the Australian government passed a new law. It was a law that gave an equal wage to all workmen: black or white. Until then Aboriginal stockmen had been paid for their work in kind: once a year some cotton working clothes, a weekly ration of flour, tea, sugar and treacle. From time to time they were allowed to butcher a bullock and share the meat among themselves and their family members. Whole families stayed on the station's lands where the Aboriginal women and children were able to search for their traditional foods. This supplementation of native foods, with that of the white men's rations was very important for their health. At this time white workers on the stations had been paid award wages, in dollars and not in goods.

The farmers objected to the new arrangement, arguing that Aboriginal workers were not as efficient as white workers. Here it is important to mention that right from the beginning, most of the workers on sheep and cattle stations who worked with animals as stockmen were Aborigines. Unfortunately this seemingly fair law spelled new hardships for the Aborigines. Most of them lost their jobs. Unemployed stockmen and their dependants drifted to government settlements where they were given a pension, which the Aborigines called "*sit down money*". The free times of the Aboriginal stockmen came to an end. Not able to live entirely off the land, they were now forced to stay in camps provided by the government.

MacDonnell Ranges – view from Papunya

Tanami Desert

To one of the desert settlements, called Papunya, came the family of Billy Stockman. It was a settlement which had started in 1959. In it, without any considerations for tribal differences, were placed people from all over central Australia and Western deserts. Tribes of Warlpiri, Luritja, Pitjandjadjarra, Anmatyerre, Aranda and Pintupi were thrown together. Never before had so many desert people camped in such a confined space. Problems between the different tribes were a common occurrence. The free people of the immense deserts were made to live in a kind of concentration camp. It was a very unfortunate decision by the law-makers.

To alleviate boredom Billy tried to find some kind of employment. At first he worked in the settlement's communal kitchen. With Clifford Possum he also repaired cars and weapons. After some time, Billy and Long Jack Phillipus became employed as handymen at the local school, where Tim Leura taught Aboriginal children traditional stories and the meaning of symbols painted on bodies during corroborees. Geoffrey Bardon, an art teacher, also taught at the school. The meeting of Billy with Bardon was the deciding factor in Billy becoming, in time, one of the most famous Aboriginal painters in Australia. In May 1971, on the advice of Geoffrey Bardon, Billy and Long Jack Phillipus helped the students to paint on the wall of the school a traditional story of the honey ant. It was the first mural painted in Papunya.

The painter

Geoffrey Bardon was the catalyst for an explosion of artistic expression among the Aboriginal men that lived in Papunya. He developed a good relationship with several men in Papunya. They were: Kappa Mbitjana Jampitjinpa, Old Mick Jagamarra, Uta Uta Jangala, Long Jack Phillipus Jagamarra, and Billy Stockman Tjapaltjarri.

In time, many more Aboriginal men began to paint their stories. Most were from the Pintupi, Warlpiri, Luritja and Anmatyerre/Western Arrente tribes. Encouraged in their endeavours by Geoffrey Bardon the men worked with newly found enthusiasm.

In 1972 the Papunya Tula Artists Company was inaugurated. It became the first Aboriginal organisation to bring together Indigenous artists and look after their interests. One of the founding members was Billy Stockman Tjapaltjarri. Since then, many exhibitions of paintings, from Papunya Tula artists have been held in cities throughout the world, such as Los Angeles, New York, London, Paris, Frankfurt, Basel, Zurich, Madrid, Montpellier, Warsaw and Moscow among many other places.

One of the early examples of Billy Stockman's work entitled "Yam Dreaming".

In the collection of Arunta Gallery.

Billy Stockman painting "CARPET SNAKE DREAMING"

The artist with his paintings

Billy Stockman Tjapaltjarri "CARPET SNAKE DREAMING"

1976 saw some fundamental changes in Government policies towards the Indigenous population. The changes were in response to the continuous uncompromising fight by the Aboriginal people for their rights, one of them being the right to own land. An end to the shameful policies of the Australian government for the assimilation of the Indigenous people culminated in the passing of a law in the Northern Territory known as the Land Rights Act. This law granted the Aborigines a right of return to their former tribal territories and the right to establish new settlements on lands that belonged to them before the coming of the white people.

Billy Stockman Tjapaltjarri painting "MEN'S CORROBOREE"

Billy Stockman Tjapaltjarri was an energetic campaigner for the outstation movement (the return to tribal lands and the establishment there of settlements). He was one of the first to establish his own outstation near Papunya, where he settled with his wife Initinika, two daughters and two sons.

In the 1970s Billy was also a member of Papunya's Town Council and Chairman of the Papunya Tula Artists. He was also a member of the Aboriginal Arts Board of the Australia Council (1975-1979) and of the National Aboriginal Conference, both Federal bodies.

Billy Stockman Tjapaltjarri. "HUNTING STORY"

Although he led an active life as a socio-political activist, Billy did not neglect his greatest passion, painting. He developed at that time his specific painting technique, using a brush to apply elongated dots that filled the composition on the surface of the canvas. Billy's reputation as a traditional Aboriginal artist, with an extraordinarily well-developed artistic sensitivity, became well established. To this day art lovers, owners of world-renowned galleries, critics and connoisseurs praise his mastery of colours and composition. Billy Stockman Tjapaltjarri paints traditional Aboriginal mythological stories. His "Dreaming" stories that belong to him and which he paints are Carpet Snake, Rainbow Snake, Spider, Budgerigar, Rain, Onion, Yam and Wild Potato.

Billy Stockman Tjapaltjarri, "RAINBOW SNAKES DREAMING"

His resolve to get to know even a small part of the world has taken Billy to some overseas destinations. He has visited the United States of America several times. In 1988 he was commissioned, together with Michael Nelson Jagamarra, to make sand paintings during the Dreamtime Exhibition at the Asia Society Gallery on Park Avenue in New York. On his return from visiting New York he said:

- ***Town's interesting… but why build such tall houses... don't they have enough space on the ground? And too much noise. Everybody runs all the time. Run, run, run… and then they get real crazy about money, all the time talk about money,... crazy about money.***

Billy Stockman Tjapaltjarri, "MEN'S CORROBOREE"

Billy Stockman Tjapaltjarri, "CEREMONY DREAMING"

Billy also visited Europe, then Papua New Guinea, New Zealand, and South Africa during the "All Black Festival". His fondest memories were of the African festival activities, but the black soils of the diamond mines made the greatest impression on him, particularly a visit to where the miners worked with the enormous dredges and trucks. Billy was very much taken with the idea of mining for diamonds and was keen to try his hand at this kind of work. He was persuaded that the art that he creates is a more valuable "diamond" than the transparent pebbles wrenched out from beneath the earth. Still, it is that visit which he recalls most often.

Billy and Initinika - "nomads".

Since the mid 1980s Billy Stockman Tjapaltjarri has lived as a "nomad". He travels between Alice Springs, Papunya and Mt.Liebig. Lately he has spent time in Mt.Liebig where his daughter Punata is in charge of the Health Centre. Punata and Billy's other daughter Gillian are both artists. Punata has designed posters about health awareness issues, Gillian more often stays in Alice Springs and paints for a local gallery owner.

In the mid 1990s Billy Stockman started to paint the traditional stories of his ancestors on much larger canvases. The larger size gave him more scope to portray the titanic battles of the Rainbow Snake and the efforts of the Dreamtime ancestors when they created the features of the landscape. While a small company was making a film about his art he painted for them a triptych called "Snake Dreaming at Mt Denison". In a masterly way he depicted the stories connected with the legends of Tjungurrayi and Tjapaltjarri men of the Anmatyerre/Aranda tribe. The men went hunting during the Dreamtime and performed ceremonies associated with the Rainbow Snake.

Billy Stockman Tjapaltjarri, "MEN'S CORROBOREE"

The very rich mythology of the Australian Aborigines consists of many legends, myths and stories. Although some of them have the same theme, they are re-told and performed differently by members of neighbouring tribes. Even tribes-people within the same community might interpret or highlight different aspect of the Dreamtime story. This can be shown, for example, in the

triptych called *Mount Denison Dreaming*. We asked the three, living Tjapaltjarri "brothers" to paint the story of Mt Denison, which in the Anmatyerre language is called *Ylpana*. Unfortunately, Tim Leura, the older brother of Clifford Possum has passed away. At this time we were producing a film about the so-called "*dot*" art of the Aboriginal artist from Central Australian deserts.

"Mt. DENISON DREAMING"

Painted by:

Clifford Possum *Billy Stockman* *Cassidy*

T J A P A L T J A R R I

Each of the brothers asked to participate in the project depicted the same legend but the characters and situations were portrayed from different perspectives. This depended on which part of the story belonged to the artist concerned and for what part of the story each of the tribal men was responsible. Billy Stockman used the centre part of the triptych to tell the story of the Rainbow Serpent; Cassidy painted Blue Kangaroo Dreaming and Clifford Possum depicted the Wallaby Dreaming at the important dreaming site at *Ylpana* (Mt. Denison).

Billy's health has declined of late because of his advancing age and he is missing his wife Initinika, who passed away. His sons and daughters now have their own families and some of them live away from Mt.Liebig. He is not such a prolific painter as he used to be and the joys of travel cannot be indulged in any more. Billy spends most of his days in a special institution for the elderly. Even here he picks up his paints and brushes and tries to paint dreamtime stories. He is a charming, friendly man who is well liked and respected. Billy has retained his sparkling sense of humour, which is very much appreciated by his friends and acquaintances.

Shared coffee. From left: Michael Hollows - gallery owner in Alice Springs and Aboriginal artists: Clifford Possum Tjapaltjarri, Billy Stockman Tjapaltjarri and Mick Namararri Tjapaltjarri.

We try to visit Billy every time we are in central Australia. It is invariably a happy time, especially if we go for a drive around Alice Springs. Being an outgoing and garrulous personality, Billy likes to keep in contact with his friends and show them he is still *"fit and well"*. One day we took Billy for a drive to the centre of Alice Springs. He wanted to shop. After we finished shopping we returned to the car and suddenly were besieged by a large group of Billy's male relations. In loud voices they demanded money from Billy. It is an Aboriginal custom

to share possessions with one's kin. They thought that Billy had sold a painting and of course they wanted their share of good fortune. With a disdaining look at the men Billy announced:

- *Today is not Billy's pay-day.*

Before Billy moved to the retirement home, he invited us to visit him in Mt.Liebig. We drove along the dusty, desert road. Before going to see Billy we stopped at the local shop to purchase some drinks for our parched throats. On leaving the shop we were stopped by an Aboriginal acquaintance with whom we chatted for a while. Suddenly Billy's raised voice could be heard coming from his small garden some distance away.

- ***Tjupurrulla, Napurrula.***

He called us by names given to us by the Aborigines.

- ***I am here! I am waiting for you!***

We quickly walked over. Billy was indignant and let us know in no uncertain manner that he was not happy with our behaviour. By not coming to him first we had ignored a common protocol and might have diminished his standing in the community. It was he who invited us and we should have come to him first. Of course we apologised profusely and promised to watch our manners in the future.

On another occasion, when we stayed with Billy for a few days, we witnessed the following incident. Billy was

frying lamb chops and steak on a small fire in the backyard, for himself and his ailing wife. While the meat was cooking in the frying pan, Billy was telling us a story. We chatted for a while. The steaks were nearly done when suddenly Billy's dogs swooped from behind the house and in a flash grabbed the sizzling pieces of meat. Billy tried to save his supper but he was too slow for the fast dogs. They simply gulped up the hot meat. He was very upset at first and blamed himself for not watching the meat more closely. The dogs went unpunished. Billy explained they probably were hungry as well and have to eat too. This is the true Billy, a kind and understanding man. The White-haired man, the Tjulkurra.

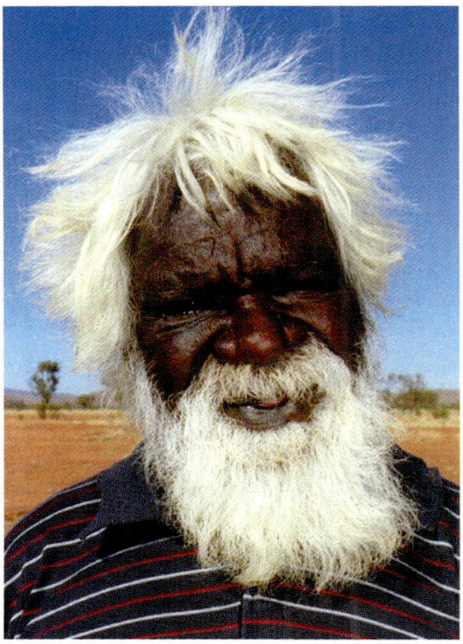

The White-haired man -The Tjulkurra.

"Desert ghost"

Bibliography & further reading:

Lacour-Gayet, R. – "***A CONCISE HISTORY OF AUSTRALIA***", Penguin Books, 1976.

Robinson, F. and York, B. – "***THE BLACK RESISTANCE***", Widescope, Camberwell,Vic., 1977.

Ward, R. – "***A NATION FOR A CONTINENT***", Heinemann Educational Australia, 1977.

Molony, J. – "***HISTORY OF AUSTRALIA***", Penguin Books, Australia,1987.

Amadio, N. and Kimber, R. – "***WILDBIRD DREAMING***" Greenhouse Publications, Melbourne, 1988.

Art Gallery of South Australia. – "***DREAMINGS OF THE DESERT***", Adelaide, 1996.

Bardon, G. – "***PAPUNYA TULA, ART OF THE WESTERN DESERT***", J.B.Books, Marleston, 1998.

Elder, B. – "***BLOOD ON THE WATTLE***", New Holland, Frenchs Forest, 1994.

Germaine, M. – "***ARTISTS & GALLERIES OF AUSTRALIA",*** Craftsman House, Roseville, 1990.

Johnson, V. – "***ABORIGINAL ARTISTS OF THE WESTERN DESERT- A BIOGRAPHICAL DICTIONARY***", Craftsman House, Roseville, 1994.

Johnson, V. – "***THE ART OF CLIFFORD POSSUM TJAPALTJARRI"***, G+B Arts International, East Roseville, 1994.

Mudrooroo. – "***MITOLOGIA ABORYGENOW***" , Dom Wydawniczy Rebis, Poznan, Poland, 1997.

Reed, A.W. – "***ABORIGINAL MYTHS – TALES OF THE DREAMTIME",*** Reed Books, Sydney, 1991.

Stanislawska-Birnberg, M. – "***JOURNEYLINES***", J.B. Books Australia, 2000.

Sturt's Desert Pea

Janusz B.Kreczmanski left Poland in 1983 and arrived in Australia from France in 1984. He began his photographic career in 1951 at the same time pursuing a tertiary education attaining a Master Degree in Film Art in 1965, Lodz, Poland. He worked in Documentary Film Studio in Warsaw, Poland 1955-1983 as director of photography and film director. Since 1984 he has been a cinematographer a professional photographer and journalist in Australia. In the course of his professional duties he filmed and took photographs in seventy- eight countries and the Hutt River Province Principality.

Margo Stanislawska-Birnberg migrated to Australia in 1963 from her native Poland. With her first husband, two small sons and her father, Martin Stanislawski, she travelled extensively throughout her new country. In the Gibson Desert, Western Australia, they met two Aborigines still leading a traditional way of life, which had not changed for thousands of years.

For Yatungka and Warri, Margo and her family were the first white people they encountered. Their travels and adventures in the Australian bush led to the making of three successful films. Margo has three sons and lives in Melbourne with her second husband. Passion for travel and the beauty of Australian remote regions inspire her writings. She is a poet, photographer and a journalist.